DEMCO

T·J·PUBLISHERS

ILLUSTRATIONS BY / FRANK ALLEN PAUL
RESEARCH ILLUSTRATOR / THE SALK INSTITUTE
LA JOLLA / CALIFORNIA

T·J·PUBLISHERS

SIGNS OF DRUG USE

AN INTRODUCTION TO DRUG AND ALCOHOL VOCABULARY IN AMERICAN SIGN LANGUAGE

BY JAMES WOODWARD

ROYALTIES

Royalties from this book will go to Sign Language Research, Inc. Sign Language Research, Inc., is a nonstock corporation established under the laws of the State of Maryland. It is new and independent from any existing institutions or organizations. Sign Language Research, Inc. has received tax-exempt status from the Internal Revenue Service. Research focus is on sign languages as they are used in Deaf communities throughout the world.

Cover and book design by FRANK ALLEN PAUL

© 1980, SIGN LANGUAGE RESEARCH, INC.

T.J. PUBLISHERS, INC.
817 Silver Spring Avenue, 305-D / Silver Spring, Maryland 20910

Printed in the United States of America

ISBN 0-932666-04-3
Library of Congress Catalog No.: 80-51369

First Printing April 1980
Second Printing March 1984

ACKNOWLEDGEMENTS

Because of the need to protect the rights of consultants, no names of Deaf individuals appear in this book. However, I do wish to thank the Deaf consultants who worked with me and the two Deaf sign models. Without their valuable assistance, this book could never have been developed.

I also wish to thank Susan De Santis for assistance in data collection in the East.

Any insensitivities or inaccuracies are my responsibility alone.

CONTENTS

INTRODUCTION 1

DRUG SIGNS, LANGUAGE ATTITUDES, AND
LANGUAGE USE 1
SOME CAUTIONS WITH DATA COLLECTION 3
SOME SOCIOLINGUISTIC VARIATIONS IN DRUG
SIGNS 5

SIGN ILLUSTRATIONS 9

ALCOHOL USE AND AFFECTS 11
CAFFEINE-RELATED DRUGS 23
DRUGS USUALLY IN PILL FORM 25

GENERAL DRUG AFFECTS   33
MARIJUANA USE AND AFFECTS   43
TOBACCO USE   53
OTHER SIGNS   57

FINGERSPELLED VOCABULARY   72

BIBLIOGRAPHY   74

SIGN INDEX   76

PERSONAL NOTES   81

INTRODUCTION

The topic of this book is of a sensitive nature. In the United States, negative value judgements are often placed on drug use and users. In addition, non drug users who are knowledgeable about drug use are often suspected to be drug users and are treated negatively.

When I first mentioned this project to a Deaf friend, her first comment was, "Oh you're collecting these signs so Hearing people can arrest more Deaf people for using drugs, huh?" This was a very reasonable suspicion because of what has happened to Deaf people in the past. However, as I explained to my friend, my intention was totally different.

The following are some of the reasons why I want to make information on drug signs available. Deaf people have been and could be involved in trials related to drug use. It is uncertain how many interpreters know drug related signs. Good drug education materials for Deaf people are lacking. Signed information on drug contaminants, such as paraquat, drug mixing dangers, etc. are not available.

I urge prospective users to handle the information in this book with sensitivity.

DRUG SIGNS, LANGUAGE ATTITUDES, AND LANGUAGE USE

Sociolinguistic attitudes must be positive, if adequate communication and interpreting services are to result. There should be respect for all languages in the communication situation. Cross cultural judgements must be avoided. Hearing people cannot judge an American Sign Language (ASL) translation of an English word the same way that they judge the English word. The sign and word belong to two different languages and value systems.

Often, Hearing people ethnocentrically consider English better than ASL and will try to invent new signs if they do not know an ASL sign for an intended meaning. However, it is much easier and more logical to ask Deaf people what the sign is. If some Deaf people do not have a sign that meets the English definition, Deaf people from other regions of the country will probably have a sign. Sometimes signs are borrowed from one sign language into another, for example, the sign VODKA that is listed in this book was borrowed from Russian Sign Language by some American signers. It is always preferable from a linguistic point of view to use existing words within a language than to try to invent new words for language standardization.

The question of ASL attitudes and use is extremely important in drug signs. As I point out in the notes a large number of drug signs are borrowed from English either through initialization, for example, QUAALUDES (1), MARIJUANA (3), JOINT (1); or through the processes of phonological and morphological modifications of fingerspelled borrowings discussed by Battison (1978), for example, LID (1), OVERDOSE.

However, even though many of these signs are borrowed from English, they are only very rarely used in English-like signing. They are rather almost always used in ASL grammatical constructions. For example, compounds, like the Noun-Adjective construction PAPER+ROLL-A-JOINT meaning "rolling paper" is ASL not English. Also ASL inflections and derivations occur with these signs. The signs TOKE, PASS-AROUND-A-JOINT, POT-PARTY, SMOKE-GRASS, POT-HEAD (1), and some others are all distinguished by ASL modulations of one sign.

The reader who wants to use these signs would be advised to associate as much as possible with Deaf individuals who use ASL as their preferred language and to read the current linguistic research on ASL grammatical structure. Two beginning suggestions are Wilbur (1979) for a summary discussion of ASL research and Klima and Bellugi (1979) for a discussion of verb modulation in ASL. If the prospective user of these signs does not follow some or all of the above suggestions, s/he runs the risk of using many of the signs in this book inappropriately. Such a use of signs may very well cause misunderstanding and communication breakdown.

SOME CAUTIONS WITH DATA COLLECTION

The only way to communicate effectively with Deaf people is to find out what language forms they use in a given community. The only way to find out is to actually talk with a number of Deaf individuals with various educational backgrounds and social roles in the community. This can be fairly easy, however, there are some pitfalls that should be avoided.

Some Deaf people are reluctant to show these signs to Hearing people. One way to approach the situation is to explain that the signs will be used for interpreting purposes, especially in court cases. To loosen things up a bit, the Hearing person should carefully try to demonstrate some of the drug signs s/he has seen, asking Deaf people if there are other signs used in the community.

Recording of such data can be dangerous for the reasons mentioned earlier in this paper. Several of the first people interviewed were apprehensive about being video-taped. I explained that the original videotape would be erased once the data was transcribed and analyzed and that I would personally keep the videotape with me at all times until the videotape could be erased. I also paid individual consultants in cash for the interviews so there would be no possibility of finding out identities of consultants through any connection with me. I think all of these precautions are justified, and I would strongly urge anyone who wants to continue research in this area to follow the same or similar procedures in protecting the identity of consultants. It is important to mention again that people who know ASL or English drug vocabulary are not necessarily users of drugs themselves. Furthermore, whether or not a consultant uses drugs (including alcohol), the researcher has no right to allow the research to expose this fact to the public but has every ethical responsibility to protect the rights and identity of the consultants.

In the collection of signs, the researcher should be sure to note the sociological characteristics of persons who use different signs. Sociolinguistic studies have found systematic variation in ASL phonology (formation), vocabulary, and grammar because of factors of social class background (Woodward 1973, 1975), region (Woodward, Erting, and Oliver 1976, Woodward and De Santis 1977a), ethnic origin (Woodward 1976, Woodward and De Santis 1977b), age (Woodward and De Santis 1977b) and sex (De Santis 1977). Deaf people of signing Deaf parents should be interviewed first, and all groups should have one or two Deaf people of Deaf parents as controls.

What I have described requires a lot of effort. But that's what communication is all about: making the effort.

While signs for drug use do not appear to undergo as much sociolinguistic variation as some other semantic domains, such as food signs and signs of sexual behavior, they still do undergo some variations. Knowing the sociolinguistic limitations on a given sign's use is as important as knowing the form of the sign itself.

SOME SOCIOLINGUISTIC VARIATIONS IN DRUG SIGNS

Signs for drug use have some interesting regional and socioethnic variations. A few of these variations are discussed below. All of the variations I have noticed are mentioned in the notes.

One example of regional variation occurs in the signs MARIJUANA (2), which is used primarily in California, and MARIJUANA (3), which is used primarily around Gallaudet College in Washington, D.C. The California variant is made on the arm, usually with a "W" handshape. The Gallaudet variant is made on the index finger, always with an "M" handshape.

As Woodward (1976, 1979) points out, Black Southern signs are less generally known to non-Black signers in the U.S., thus when other signers see a Black Southern sign, they often misunderstand or misinterpret it. The Black Louisiana sign for WHISKEY, BEER, WINE looks like the commonly used White sign for DRINK-ALCOHOL, except the Black sign uses a "Y" instead of an "A" handshape.

An example of age variation occurs in the sign WHISKEY: the form with two different handshapes is the older form, and the form with the same (assimilated) handshape is the newer form. Sometimes people of one generation will not immediately catch a form from a different generation. Thus it is important to be aware of historical age variations when choosing which sign or form of a sign to use.

There are also important interrelationships between regional, ethnic, and age variations. For example, Southern signers tend to use older forms of signs more often than do non-Southern signers, and Blacks in the South tend to use historically older forms more than Whites (Woodward and Erting 1975, Woodward 1976, Woodward and De Santis 1977b). Following this same trend, the older unassimilated form of WHISKEY tends to be used more by Southerners than by non-Southerners and more by Blacks in the South than by Whites.

If Hearing people, especially interpreters, want to establish effective communication with Deaf individuals, they will endeavor to learn what signs are being used by *all* aspects of the Deaf community that they come into contact with. In the notes included with each sign, I have listed all of the regional, ethnic, style, and age variations that I am familiar with for the signs presented. It is crucial that these notes be used when studying these signs.

SIGN ILLUSTRATIONS

Notes on the signs collected for drug use appear with each drawing. These notes should be used in conjunction with the sign drawings. Several cautions about these signs must be made here again. THESE ARE ONLY *SOME* SIGNS FOR DRUG USE. THEY DO NOT INCLUDE ALL SIGNS FOR DRUG USE OR ALL VARIANTS. THEY MAY OR MAY NOT BE USED IN A GIVEN COMMUNITY. IT IS THE RESPONSIBILITY OF THE PERSON USING THIS BOOK TO FIND WHAT IS BEING USED IN A GIVEN COMMUNITY.

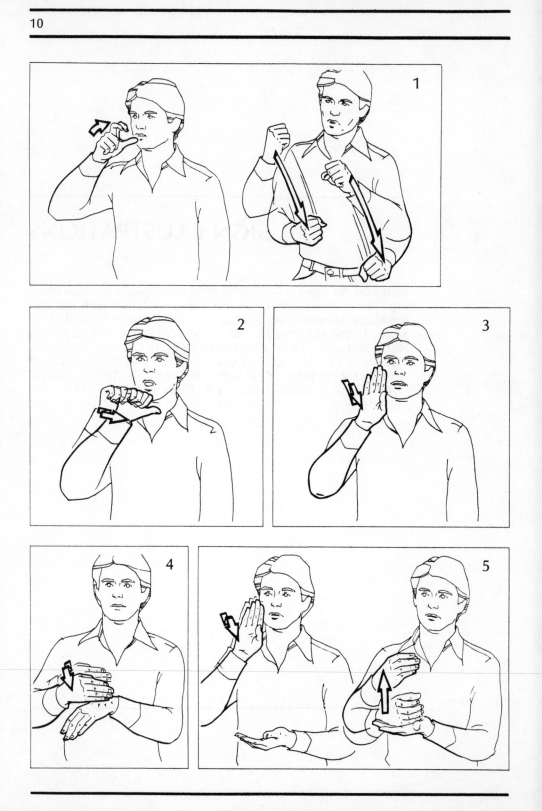

ALCOHOL USE AND AFFECTS

1 ALCOHOLIC

This is a compound of DRINK-COCKTAIL + STRONG (modulated). Note that STRONG (modulated) also occurs in POT-HEAD (SIGN 101) AND CHAIN-SMOKE (sign 116).

2 BAR (1)

This sign is derived from the sign DRINK-LIQUOR (sign 13). Note the small repeated movement. Some people use the same hand orientation as DRINK-LIQUOR; others change the orientation as shown in this illustration.

3 BEER (1)

This is the more commonly used variant.

4 BEER (2)

This is less commonly used than BEER (1).

5 BEER-CAN

This is a compound of BEER + SHORT-CYLINDRICAL-CONTAINER.

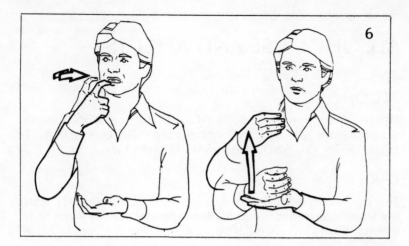

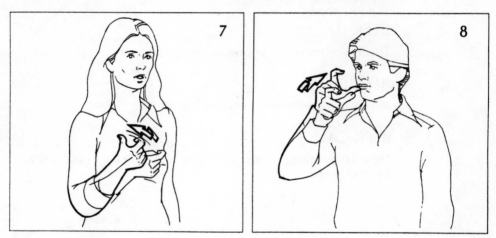

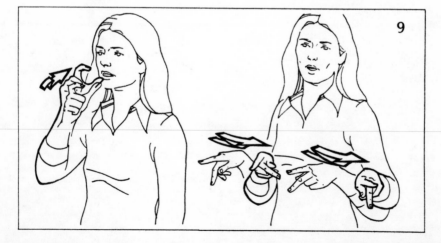

6 BOTTLE

This is a compound of GLASS + TALL-CYLINDRICAL-CONTAINER and can be compounded with BEER, WINE, etc. to indicate the type of beverage. Often when the sign for the beverage is included, the sign for GLASS may be deleted.

7 CHAMPAGNE

Sometimes this sign is used with the sign WHISKEY (sign 31) to also mean CHAMPAGNE. Other signers may make this sign holding contact on the tip of a non-dominant "1" handshape.

8 COCKTAIL, MIXED-DRINK

This is a very commonly used sign. Note the handshape is different from the sign DRINK (with a "C" handshape).

9 COCKTAIL-PARTY

This is a compound of COCKTAIL + PARTY.

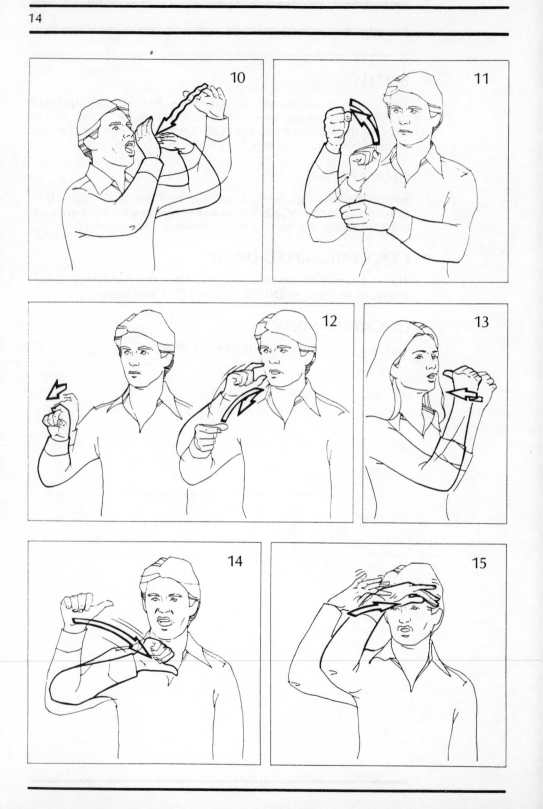

10 DOWN-A-BOTTLE, CHUG

This sign means to finish drinking a liquid without stopping.

11 DRAFT-BEER

This was the only variant found during this research.

12 DRINK-A-SHOT

This is a compound of SHOT + DRINK-A-SHOT.

13 DRINK-LIQUOR

This sign can also be done with a "Y" handshape. For the sign LIQUOR-STORE, combine the signs DRINK-LIQUOR and STORE. To convey the meaning HANGOVER, sign DRINK-LIQUOR (pause) + NEXT MORNING and either THROW-UP, HEADACHE, or DIZZY.

14 DRUNK (1), BOMBED (1), PLASTERED (1), SMASHED (1)

This is the most common sign for these meanings. It may also be done with a "Y" handshape and may be one-handed or two-handed.

15 DRUNK (2), BOMBED (2), PLASTERED (2), SMASHED (2)

This is another variant for these meanings.

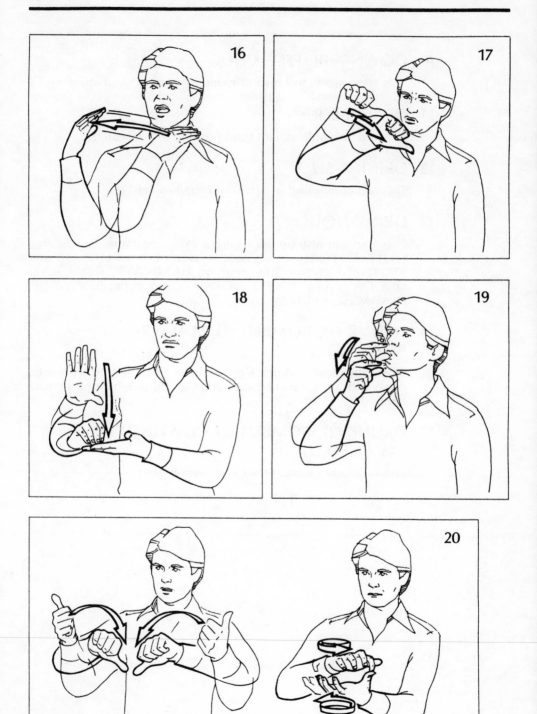

16 DRUNK (3), BOMBED (3), PLASTERED (3), SMASHED (3)

This is another variant for these meanings. This sign is slightly more emphatic than the previous variants and could be translated 'really wiped'.

17 DRUNK (noun), DRUNKARD, WINO, LUSH

This sign is derived from DRUNK (sign 14) by repeating the movement. There is also a slight change in facial expression.

18 FINISH-OFF-A-BOTTLE, FINISH-OFF-A-GLASS

This sign does not indicate anything about the time required to complete the act being described.

19 LIQUEUR

This sign can also be a compound of SWEET and LIQUEUR. Some signers will also extend the little finger for the sign LIQUEUR. Note the slight head tilt back and return.

20 MIX-DRINKS

This is a compound of POUR (modulated) + MIX.

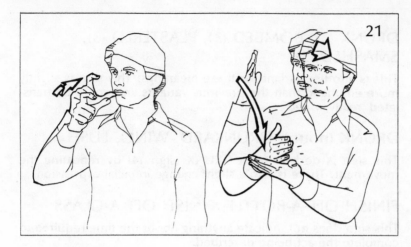

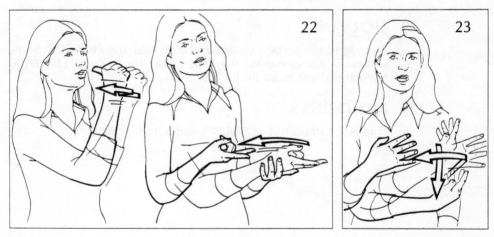

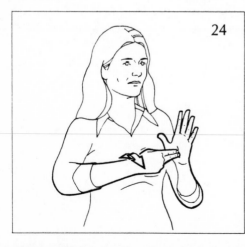

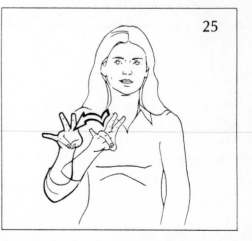

21 ON-THE-WAGON

This is a compound of COCKTAIL + STOP.

22 PASS-OUT

This sign means to pass out from liquor. It is a compound of DRINK-LIQUOR + LIE-ON-FLOOR (emphatic). One can also make other compounds utilizing the second part of this sign, for example, SMOKE-GRASS + LIE-ON-FLOOR (emphatic).

23 SCOTCH

This is the sign for SCOTLAND and in a "drinking alcohol" context takes on the extended meaning SCOTCH.

24 SCREWDRIVER

This sign, like most other names for mixed drinks, is a literal translation of the English word for the drink.

25 SEVEN-AND-SEVEN

This is like a fingerspelled word that has become a sign. Note the change to a downward orientation of the hands.

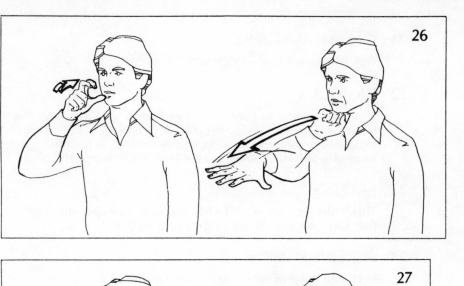

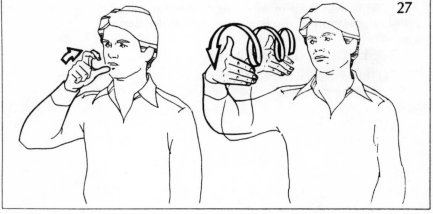

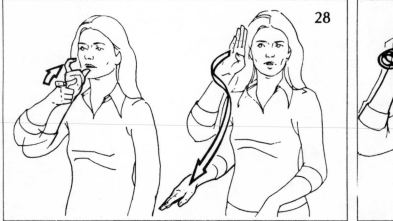

26 SOBER

This word is often translated COCKTAIL + NOTHING, when sober is used to mean 'has abstained from drinking'.

27 SOCIAL-DRINKER

This is a compound of DRINK-COCKTAIL + FROM-TIME-TO-TIME.

28 TEETOTALER

This is a compound of DRINK-COCKTAIL + NEVER.

29 TIPSY

Note the facial expression of this sign. The sign DIZZY requires a different, more intense expression and can be signed with one or two hands and a larger movement.

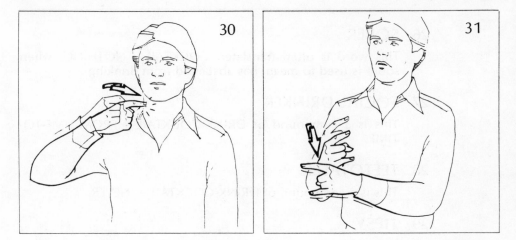

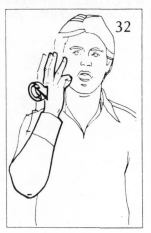

30 VODKA

This is the Russian sign for VODKA. Some American signers, primarily those on the East coast around Gallaudet College, have borrowed and use this sign.

31 WHISKEY, ALCOHOL, LIQUOR

Some signers make a distinction between WHISKEY (made with a larger, sharper movement) and LIQUOR (made with smaller, softer movements). Older signers, Southern signers, and especially Black Southern signers tend to use the older variant of this sign which has an "A" or "B" handshape on the non-dominant hand.

32 WINE

This variant, with the palm facing the cheek, is most commonly used. Some signers may vary the orientation of the hand, for example, palm facing back. Other signers may vary the point of contact, touching the fingertips of the "W" hand to the cheek.

CAFFEINE-RELATED DRUGS

33 CAFFEINE

This is a compound of DRINK + BECOME-WIDE-AWAKE. Some signers prefer to fingerspell C-A-F-F-E-I-N-E.

34 COCA-COLA, COKE

This sign is similar to SHOOT-UP (sign 153). However, this sign is made higher on the arm and only has a wiggling movement of the thumb.

35 COFFEE

This is a very commonly used sign.

36 PEPSI

This sign can be the same or different as the sign for ITALIAN. Some people sign ITALIAN in the same way and others will use a variant of ITALIAN that has a more cross-like movement.

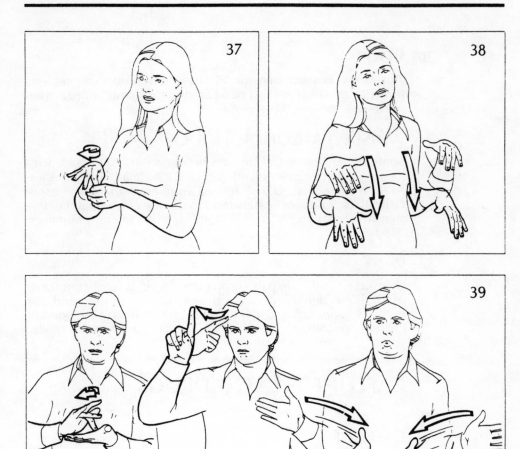

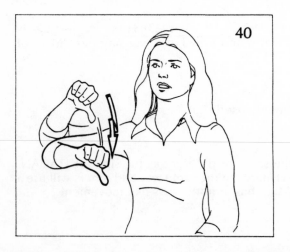

37 TEA

This is a very common sign.

DRUGS USUALLY IN PILL FORM

38 DEPRESSANT

This sign may also occur in the compound PILL + DEPRESSANT.

39 DIET-PILLS

This is commonly translated as MEDICINE + FOR + BECOME-SLIM. Another possible combination of signs is LOSE-WEIGHT (repeated movement) + MEDICINE. Other signers prefer to fingerspell "D-I-E-T P-I-L-L-S".

40 DOWNERS

Note the repeated movement in this sign. This meaning can be expressed by this sign alone or by signing PILL first.

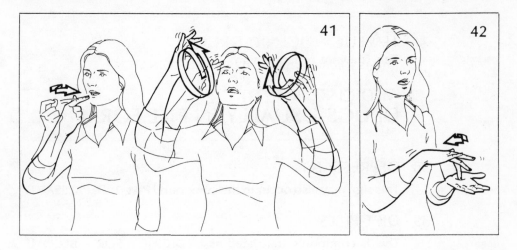

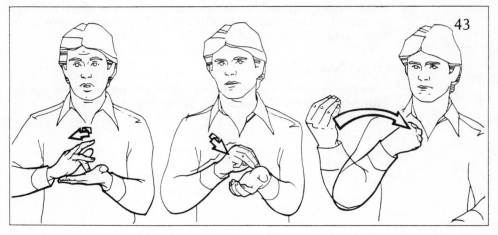

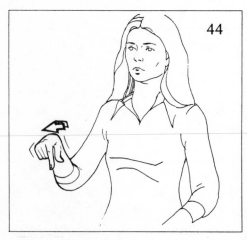

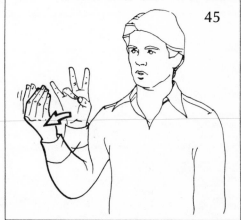

41 HALLUCINOGENIC-DRUG

This is a compound of PILL + HALLUCINATE.

42 MEDICINE, PILLS (3)

This sign generally refers to pills that are used for medical purposes.

43 PRESCRIPTION-DRUG

This is often translated as MEDICINE (pause) +
DOCTOR + GIVE-ME (directional). Note the facial expression
during the sign MEDICINE and the pause after it, indicating top-
icalization.

44 QUAALUDES (1)

This meaning can be expressed by this sign alone or by signing
PILL first.

45 QUAALUDES (2)

This meaning can also be expressed by this sign alone or by
signing PILL first. This sign is used more in California than in the
East.

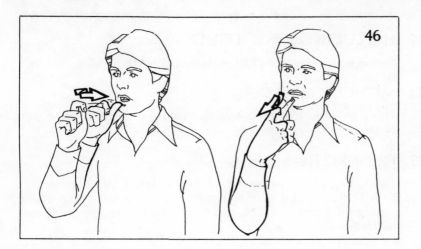

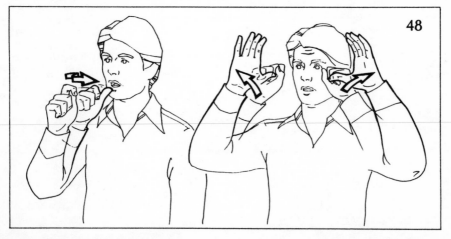

46 REDS

This sign is obviously borrowed from English. Adding the sign PILL is optional.

47 SLEEPING-PILLS

This is a compound of SLEEP (modulated) + PILL.

48 SPEED, AMPHETAMINES, BENNIES

This is a compound of PILL + BECOME-WIDE-AWAKE.

49 STIMULANT, STIMULATE

Facial expression is very important to distinguish this sign from other signs that are similar in manual movement, such as SEXUAL-EXCITEMENT and HOT-FLASHES. (See Woodward 1979 for illustrations of these signs). This sign may also occur in the compound PILL and this sign.

50 TAKE-PILL (1)

This is a commonly used sign for TAKE-PILL. The noun PILLS (1) is derived by repeating and shortening the movement.

51 TAKE-PILL (2)

This is another commonly used sign. The noun PILLS (2) is derived by shortening and repeating the movement.

52 TRANQUILIZERS

This is a compound of PILL + RELAXED.

53 UPPERS

Note the repeated movement in this sign. This meaning can be expressed by this sign alone or by signing PILL first.

54 WHITES (1)

This sign is obviously borrowed from English. The sign PILL can be optionally added before this sign.

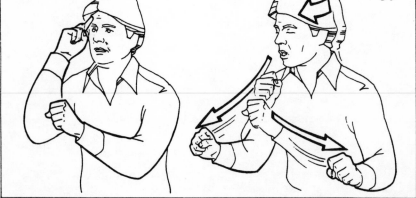

55 WHITES (2)

This variant is used more in California than in the East.

GENERAL DRUG AFFECTS

56 ADDICTED, HOOKED-ON

This is a very commonly used variant. Some signers make contact on the outside of the mouth instead of inside. To specify the type of addiction, sign the type of drug first.

57 BECOME-HEAVILY-INVOLVED-IN

The meaning of this sign is not as strong as ADDICTED, but is used to indicate that there is a heavy involvement. Sign the type of drug first.

58 BLACK-OUT (1), FAINT (1)

This is a compound of MIND and FADE-OUT (emphatic).

59 BLACK-OUT (2), FAINT (2)

This is another compound variant for this meaning.

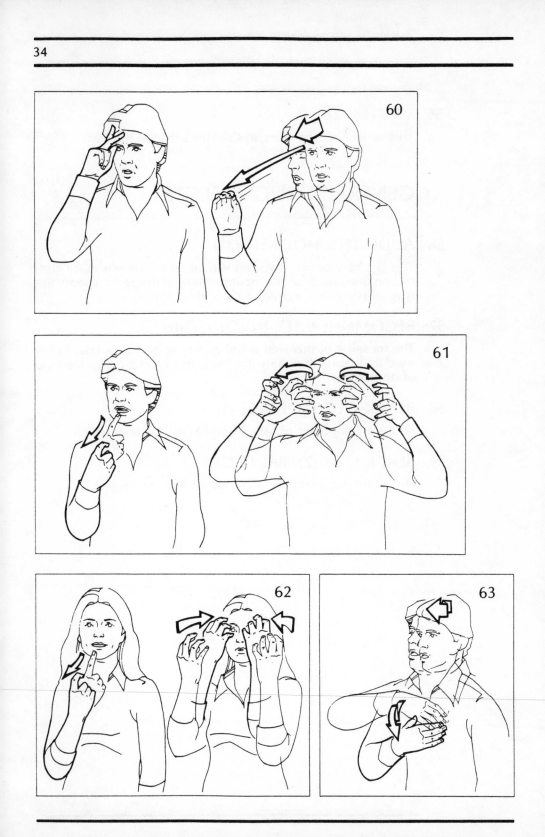

60 BLACK-OUT (3), FAINT (3)

This is an example of a fingerspelled word that has become a sign in ASL through changes in movement and location. (See Battison 1978).

61 BLOODSHOT-EYES (1)

This is a very common compound of RED + VEINS-ACROSS-EYEBALLS.

62 BLOODSHOT-EYES (2)

This is another very common compound of RED + IRRITATED-EYEBALLS.

63 COUGH (1)

This is the most commonly used variant.

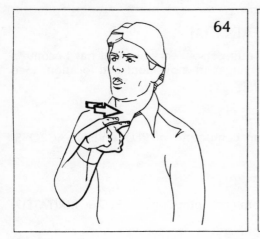

64

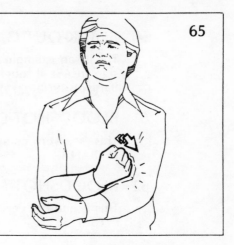

65

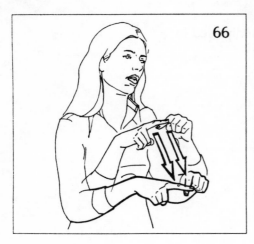

66

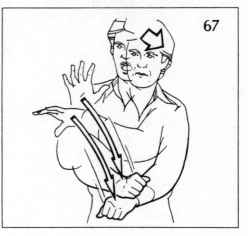

67

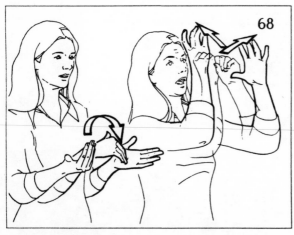

68

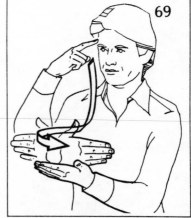

69

64 COUGH (2)

This is a less commonly used variant.

65 DRUG-DEPENDENCE (1)

This is a modulated form of DRUGS (sign 137).

66 DRUG-DEPENDENCE (2)

Name the type of drug and then use this sign. This sign is more English-related than the previous sign.

67 DRUG-HABIT

Name the type of drug and then use this sign.

68 FLASHBACK (1)

This is a compound of AGAIN + VISUALIZE-MENTALLY.

69 FREAK-OUT

This is a compound of MIND + DEVIATE.

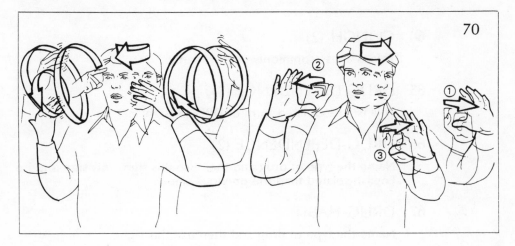

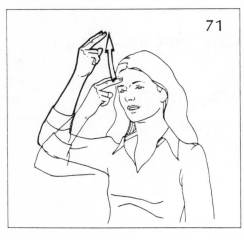

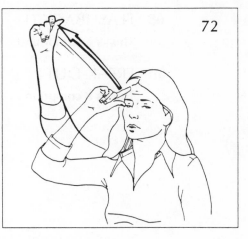

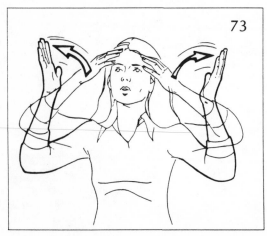

70 HALLUCINATE

This is a very common variant. The last part of the sign is sometimes used to translate DT's, especially if it is combined with the sign for DRINK-LIQUOR (sign 13). The sign FLASHBACK (2) can also be made by signing AGAIN + HALLUCINATE.

71 HIGH-FROM-DRUGS (1)

This sign is usually accompanied by an exhaling of air. It has a fairly strong relationship to English. Note the initialized handshape and the English semantic range of "high". However, the sign still has preserved some ASL morphological characteristics, since the sign is done at the head, not in the central signing space.

72 HIGH-FROM-DRUGS (2)

This sign is also usually accompanied by an exhaling of air. It has a slightly stronger connotation than the previous sign. It comes from a compound of MIND + GONE. The intensity of the high is shown through non-manual expression in ASL.

73 HIGH-FROM-DRUGS (3)

This comes from a compound of MIND + OPEN. The intensity of the high is shown through non-manual expression. For example, compare this sign with SPACED-OUT (sign 79). This sign is also normally accompanied by an exhaling of air.

74 LOADED

This is an initialized sign, used primarily in California. It can also be made on a flat "B" handshape instead of on the arm.

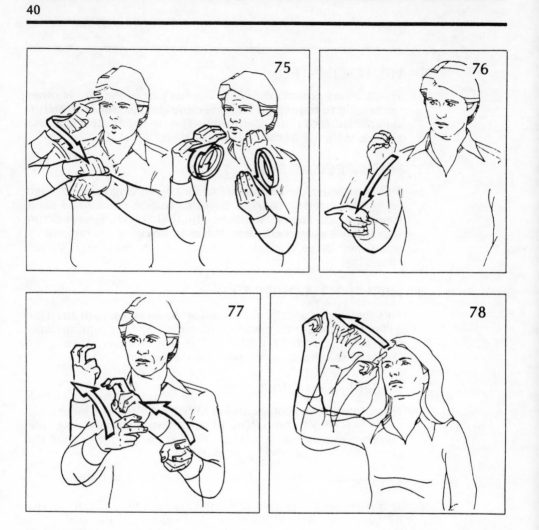

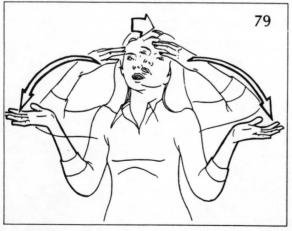

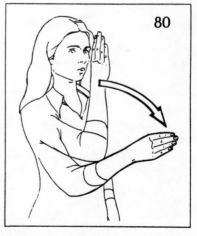

75 MUNCHIES

This is a compound of STONED + EAT (modulated). Another combination of signs for this meaning is STONED + WANT + EAT (modulated). There are several other modulations of EAT that could be used in this context.

76 OVERDOSE, O.D.

This is a fingerspelled word that has become a sign through changes in handshape and movement. (See Battison 1978). It may be compounded with the sign LIE-ON-FLOOR (sign 22) or with DIE, whichever is the appropriate meaning.

77 SICK-FROM-OVERDOSE

This is a compound of OVERDOSE and a sign that is normally translated as ANIMAL-DIE. In this particular compound, however, the sign does not mean that the person died, only that s/he is very sick. One can also add the sign DIE, if the person actually does die later.

78 SPACED-OUT (1)

This is a common sign. It could be used to translate the English 'spaced out', 'zonked', 'superstoned', etc.

79 SPACED-OUT (2)

This is another common sign that has similar meanings to the previous sign. This sign is similar to HIGH-ON-DRUGS (sign 73).

80 STRAIGHT

This sign can mean 'straight' in the drug-related or in the sexual sense.

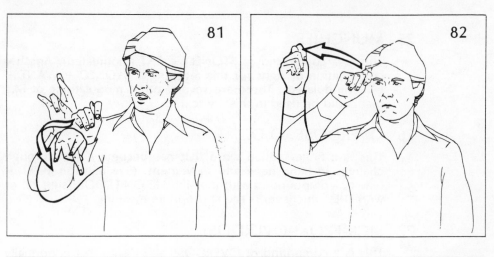

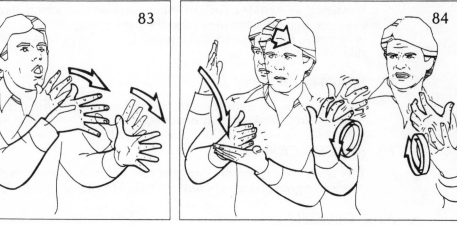

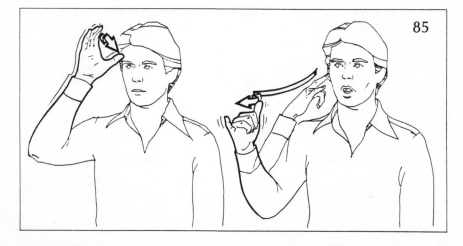

81 TRIP (1)

This is a fingerspelled borrowing from English that is becoming a sign through modifications of handshape and movement. (See Battison 1978). BAD-TRIP is signed by adding BAD before this sign.

82 TRIP (2)

This initialized variant is less common than the previous variant.

83 VOMIT, THROW-UP

This sign may also be done with one hand only.

84 WITHDRAWAL-SYMPTOMS

This is a compound of STOP + NERVOUS-IRRITATION. During the second sign the fingers should wiggle.

MARIJUANA USE AND AFFECTS

85 COLOMBIAN, COLOMBIAN-GOLD

This is a compound of the signs COLOMBIAN + GOLD. The movement of COLOMBIAN may vary in different areas. This can also be fingerspelled "C-G".

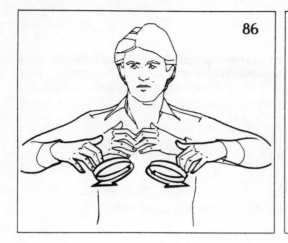

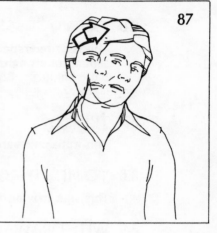

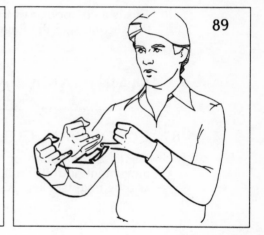

86 CLEAN-GRASS

This is a verb sign meaning 'to clean grass'. It can also be compounded with the sign MARIJUANA.

87 DO-YOU-WANT-TO-SMOKE-GRASS

This is a totally non-manual sign, used in situations where privacy of communication is desired. There is a double inhaling movement in the sign.

88 JOINT (1)

This is a common initialized variant for JOINT.

89 JOINT (2)

This sign is used sometimes in the East.

90 KILO

This sign, meaning BOX, can also be compounded with a variant of the signs for marijuana or whatever other drug is being referred to. Other signers prefer to fingerspell K-I-L-O.

91 LID (1)

This is an example of a fingerspelled word that is becoming a sign through modifications of handshape. (See Battison 1978). Note that the arms remains stationary while producing these handshapes and that the movement only envolves the thumb and index finger. Sometimes this sign is repeated.

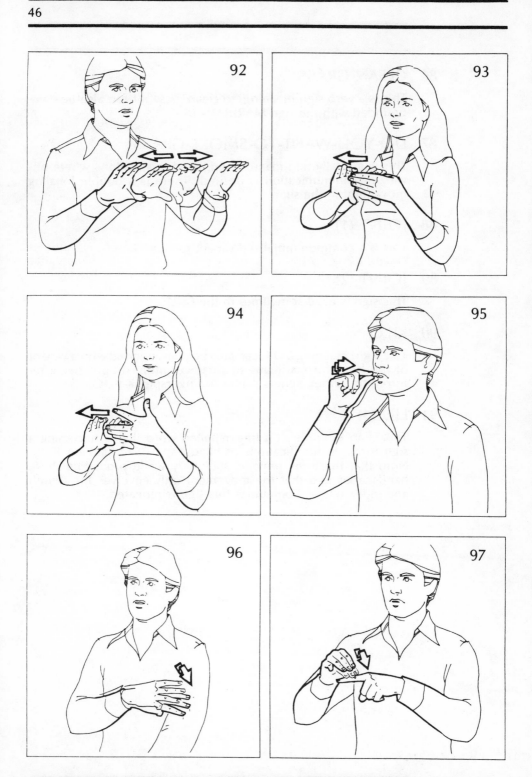

92 LID (2)

This sign can also be compounded with MARIJUANA (1), (2), or (3).

93 LID-SIZE (whole)

This sign is used to refer to the size of the lid being discussed.

94 LID-SIZE (partial)

This form is derived from the previous sign. In the East some signers bend the index finger on the base hand. One may also indicate an even smaller amount by only grasping the ring and little fingers. However, no signers interviewed had a variant that only grasped the little finger, so be careful not to overgeneralize.

95 MARIJUANA (1), GRASS (1), POT (1), WEED (1), DOPE (1)

This is the most common variant. This is a noun derived from the verb sign SMOKE-GRASS. This sign may also be done with an "F" handshape.

96 MARIJUANA (2), GRASS (2), POT (2), WEED (2), DOPE (2)

This is a commonly used initialized variant. It is not as common as MARIJUANA (1). This sign may also be done with an "M" handshape.

97 MARIJUANA (3), GRASS (3), POT (3), WEED (3), DOPE (3)

This initialized sign is primarily used around Gallaudet College. It is based on the sign CIGARETTE (sign 120).

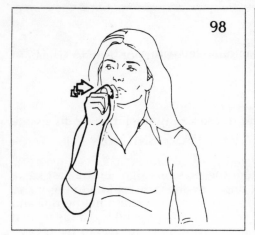

98

99

100

101

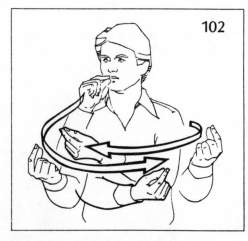

102

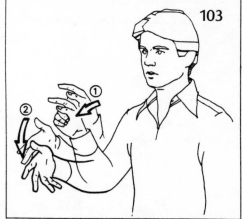

103

98 MARIJUANA (4)

This sign is only used by signers who do not use marijuana.

99 PASS-JOINT-AROUND

This is a very commonly used sign.

100 POT-HEAD (1), HEAVY GRASS SMOKER (1)

This variant is a modulated form of SMOKE-GRASS (sign 111). This type of modulation also occurs in other signs with similar semantic ranges, for example, CHAIN-SMOKE (sign 115). It can also be signed with two hands.

101 POT-HEAD (2), HEAVY GRASS SMOKER (2)

This is a compound of SMOKE-GRASS + STRONG (modulated). The second part of this compound can also be found in other signs with similar semantic ranges, for example, CHAIN-SMOKE (sign 116).

102 POT-PARTY

This is a modulated form of PASS-JOINT-AROUND.

103 ROACH (1)

This is a compound of SMALL-PART-OF-JOINT + LEAVE.

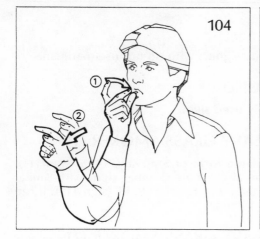

104

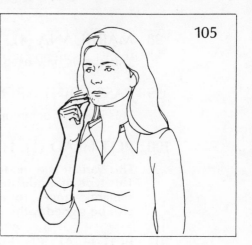

105

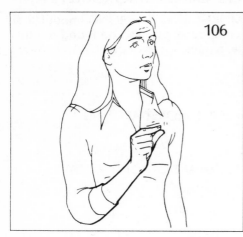

106

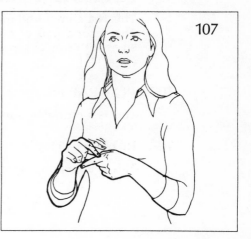

107

108

109

104 ROACH (2)

This is a compound of SMOKE-CIGARETTE-DOWN + SMALL-PART-OF-JOINT.

105 ROACH-CLIP (1)

This is a commonly used variant.

106 ROACH-CLIP (2)

This variant seems to be used more often when asking if someone has a clip.

107 ROACH-CLIP (3)

This variant is not as widely used as ROACH-CLIP (1) and (2). This variant is related to MARIJUANA (sign 97).

108 ROACH-CLIP (4)

This is an example of a fingerspelled word that is becoming a sign in ASL with certain deletions of handshape and addition of movement. (See Battison 1978).

109 ROLL-A-JOINT

This was the only variant found during this research.

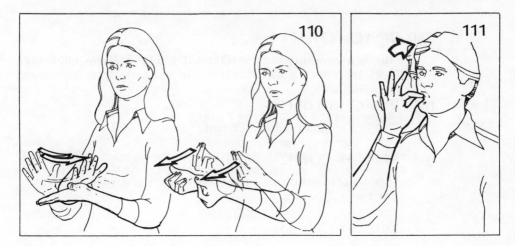

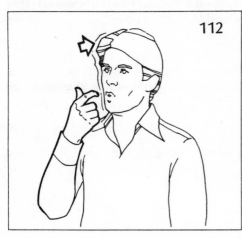

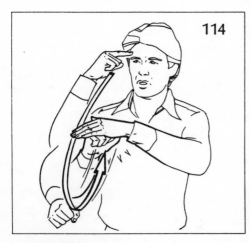

110 ROLLING-PAPER

This is a compound of the sign for PAPER + ROLL-A-JOINT (sign 109). In conversational context, the last part of the compound may be deleted.

111 SMOKE-GRASS, TOKE, HIT

Note the single head movement on this sign. Compare with MARIJUANA (sign 95), the first part of the compound POT-HEAD (sign 101), and the modulated form in POT-HEAD (sign 100). This sign may also be done with a "baby O" handshape.

112 SMOKE-MARIJUANA-PIPE

This sign refers only to smoking marijuana and requires a sucking in of air through pursed lips. The noun MARIJUANA-PIPE is derived from this sign by using small repeated movement of the hand to and from the mouth.

113 STONED (1)

This variant has a relationship to English. It is a compound of MIND + STONE.

114 STONED (2)

This is another common variant. It is a compound of MIND + HEAD-HIT-THE-CEILING. For some signers, it carries a stronger intensity than STONED (1).

TOBACCO USE

115 CHAIN-SMOKE (1), HEAVY-SMOKER (1)

This variant is a modulated form of SMOKE-CIGARETTE (sign 122). It may also be signed with one hand. This type of modulation also occurs in other signs with similar semantic ranges, for example, POT-HEAD (sign 100).

54

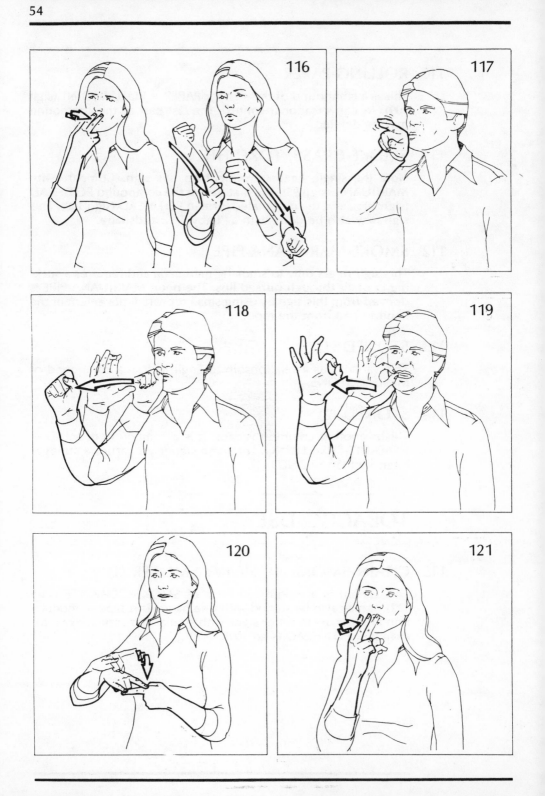

116 CHAIN-SMOKE (2), HEAVY-SMOKER (2)

This is a compound. The second part of this compound can also be found in other signs with similar semantic ranges, for example, POT-HEAD (sign 101).

117 CIGAR (1)

This is the most commonly used variant.

118 CIGAR (2)

This is a less commonly used variant.

119 CIGAR (3)

This is also a less commonly used variant. It may also be done with an "O" handshape.

120 CIGARETTE (1)

This is a commonly used variant.

121 CIGARETTE (2)

This is a commonly used variant that is derived from SMOKE-CIGARETTE (sign 122). Note the typical short, repeated noun movement.

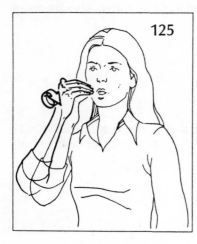

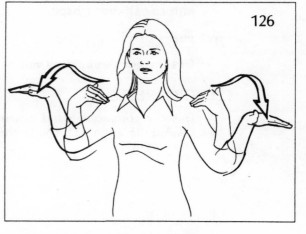

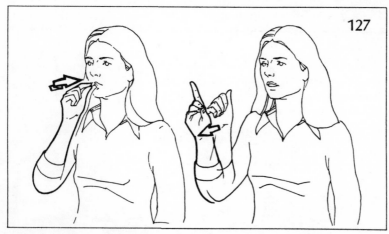

122 SMOKE-CIGARETTE

Note the difference in movement between this sign and its noun pair CIGARETTE (sign 121).

123 SMOKE-TOBACCO-PIPE (1)

This sign refers only to tobacco pipes and requires a puffing mouth movement similar to the act of puffing on a real pipe. The noun TOBACCO-PIPE (1) is derived from this sign by using small repeated movement of the hand to and from the mouth and eliminating the puffing action.

124 SMOKE-TOBACCO-PIPE (2)

This sign also refers only to tobacco pipes and requires a puffing mouth movement. TOBACCO-PIPE (2) is derived in the same manner as mentioned in the previous note.

125 TOBACCO

In different areas, there may be variation in movement and between contact with the fingertips or the knuckles. Some signers may also use an "M" handshape. This sign may be compounded with the sign CHEW to mean CHEWING-TOBACCO.

OTHER SIGNS

126 ANGEL-DUST (1), PCP (1), WACK (1), CRYSTAL (1)

This sign is directly translated from English. It is a combination of the sign ANGEL plus fingerspelling "D-U-S-T". A number of signers prefer to spell "P-C-P".

127 ANGEL-DUST (2), PCP (2), WACK (2), CRYSTAL (2)

This variant is used more in the West than in the East. It is a compound of SMOKE and fingerspelled "A-D". Signs such as SNORT can be used in place of SMOKE, although SMOKE is more common. One may also find "A-D-M" for the second part of this sign or used alone. ADM refers to a mixture of Angel Dust and Marijuana.

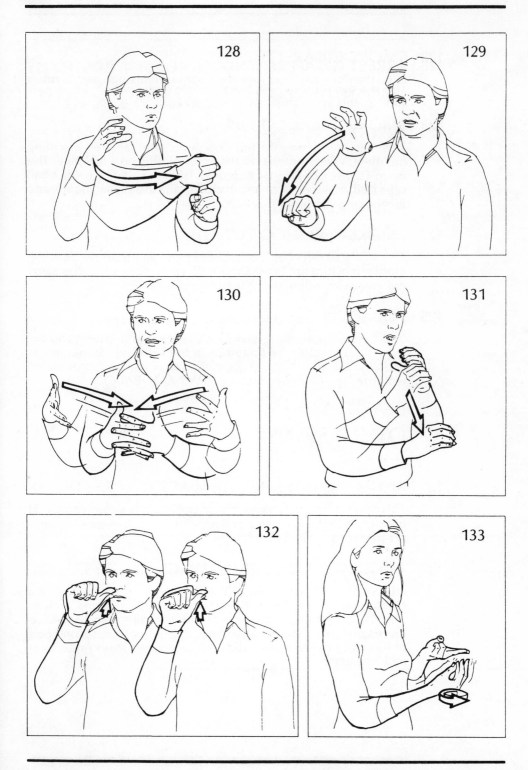

128 ARREST (1), APPREHEND (1), BUST (1), BUSTED (1)

This is a common variant. Note the use of the classifier for "person" in this sign. This variant usually means a single arrest.

129 ARREST (2), APPREHEND (2), BUST (2), BUSTED (2)

This is another common variant for the meaning of single arrest.

130 ARREST, APPREHEND, BUST, BUSTED(GROUP)

This sign would be used for a "group-arrest" or a "bust" occurring because of a police raid. This sign is similar to one of the variants for PREGNANT in ASL (See Woodward 1979). However PREGNANT has a slightly more circular movement before the hands make contact.

131 BONG

This sign can also be compounded with a variant of the signs for marijuana or hash.

132 COCAINE, COKE

Actually this sign means 'a drug that is snorted'. The usual reference, however, is COCAINE. This sign is derived from SNORT (sign 156).

133 COOK-HEROIN

This is the incorporated compound BOIL-IN-A-SPOON.

134

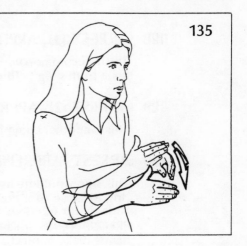

135

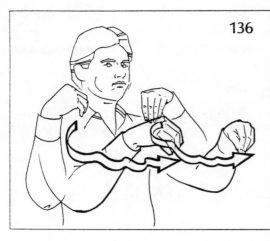

136

137

138

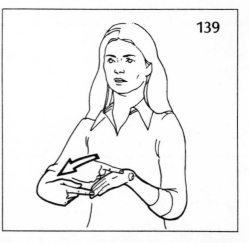

139

134 CUT(-DRUGS-WITH-OTHER-SUBSTANCE)

This is the ASL sign MIX. In a drug context, this sign means to mix a pure drug with a neutral substance to weaken it.

135 CUT-HASH

Fingerspelled "H-A-S-H" may be compounded with this sign.

136 DEAL(-IN-DRUGS), PUSH(-DRUGS)

This sign is a modulated form of the verb SELL and in the drug context can have the extended meaning of 'to deal' or 'to push drugs'. The signs DEALER and PUSHER are often signed SELL (un-modulated) + INDIVIDUAL.

137 DRUGS, NARCOTICS, HEROIN (1), SMACK (1), HORSE (1)

This sign is derived from SHOOT-UP (sign 152) by repeated movement. It is used as a general sign for DRUGS, no matter if they are injected, taken as pills, smoked, or snorted. It is also the preferred translation of HEROIN. This sign may also be used to translate ADDICT or JUNKIE.

138 HASH-OIL (1)

One can fingerspell "H-A-S-H" and then use this incorporated compound of POUR-ON-CIGARETTE.

139 HASH-OIL (2)

This is a less commonly used variant. One can fingerspell H-A-S-H and then use this sign which means APPLY-ON-CIGARETTE-PAPER.

140

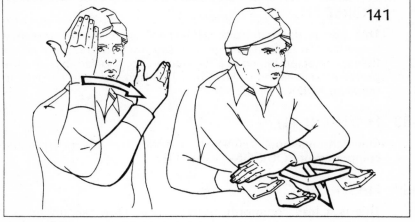

141

142

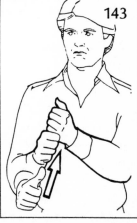

143

140 HOOKA, WATER-PIPE

This was the only variant found in this research.

141 ILLICIT(-DRUG)-DEALINGS

The sign for a specific drug and the sign SELL can be added before these signs.

142 INCENSE

This is a compound of SMELL + STICK-GIVING-OFF-SMOKE.

143 INSERT(A-DRUG)-ANALLY

This was the only variant found during the research.

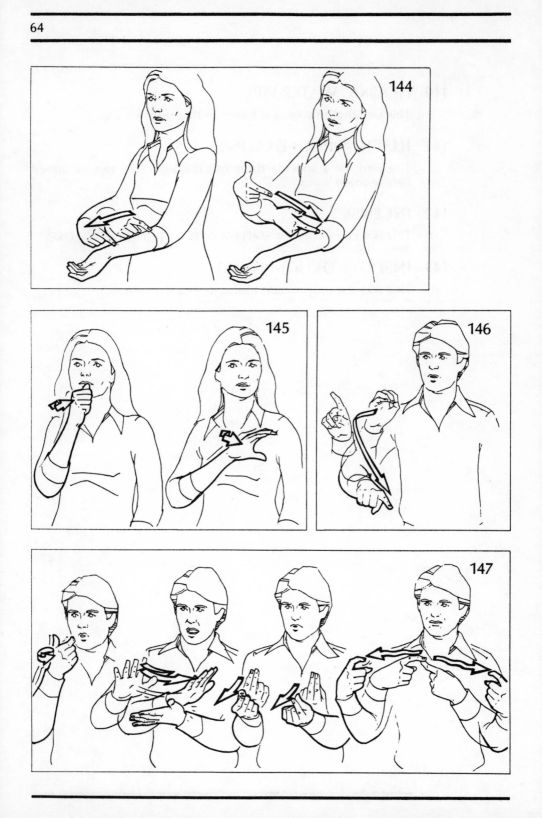

144 MAINLINE

This is a compound of VEIN + INJECT-INTO-VEIN.

145 NARCOTICS OFFICER, NARC

This is a compound of PRIVATE + POLICE. Some signers prefer to fingerspell "N-A-R-C".

146 OUNCE

This is an example of a fingerspelled word that has become a sign through modifications of handshape and movement. (See Battison 1978).

147 PARAPHERNALIA

PARAPHERNALIA is a compound of the signs PIPE + PAPERS + ROLL-A-JOINT + ETC. HEAD SHOP would be signed STORE + PARAPHERNALIA.

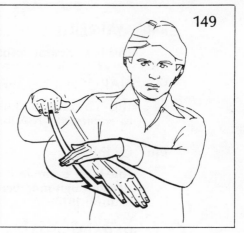

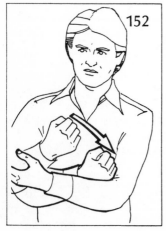

148 POPPER

While making this sign, inhale through the nose. This sign may vary considerably from one area to another.

149 RAID

This is an emphatic form of the sign ENTER.

150 SCALE (large)

This sign is used for a scale that is usually used to weigh large and/or heavier amounts.

151 SCALE (small)

This sign is used for a scale that is usually used to weigh small amounts.

152 SHOOT-UP (1)

The verb SHOOT-UP is made with a single movement.

153 SHOOT-UP (2)

This is the preferred variant for SHOOT-UP and also uses a single movement. This is a less commonly used variant for the meanings HEROIN (2), SMACK (2), and HORSE (2). (Compare with sign 137). Remember that these nouns require shorter repeated movements. The noun HYPODERMIC-NEEDLE (1) is derived in the same manner.

154 SHOOT-UP (3)

This is a less commonly used variant for SHOOT-UP. With short repeated movements, this sign may also be translated as HEROIN (3), SMACK (3), HORSE (3), and HYPODERMIC-NEEDLE (2).

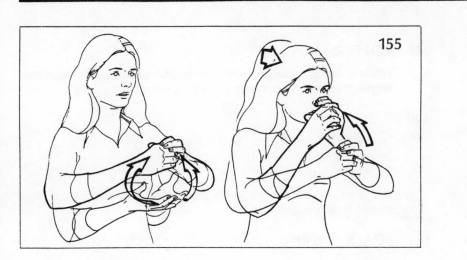

155

156

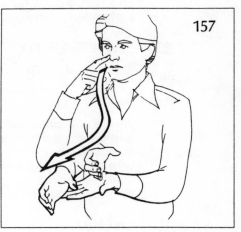

157

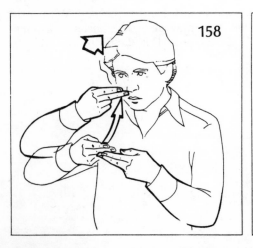

158

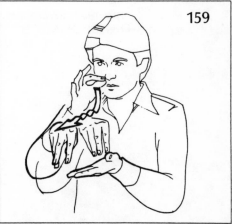

159

155 SNIFF-GLUE, GLUE-SNIFFING

This is a compound of BAG + INHALE-FROM-BAG. Not many people use this sign now, since the ingredients of glue have been changed.

156 SNORT

This is the most common sign for SNORT. It may also be done with an "I" (palm up) or an "F" handshape. Breath is drawn in through the nose during the production of the sign.

157 SNORT-A-LINE

This is a compound sign. It means to snort through the nose a line of drug in powdered form.

158 SNORT-FROM-SPOON

This variant is a verb when done with one movement. The nouns SNORTING-SPOON and COKE-SPOON are derived from the verb by shortening and repeating the movement.

159 SNORT-WITH-STRAW (1)

This was one variant with this meaning found during this research.

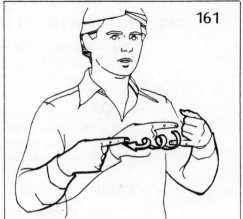

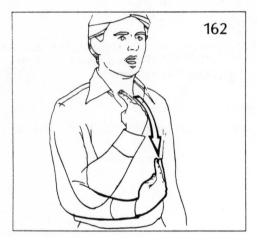

160 SNORT-WITH-STRAW (2)

While making this sign tilt the head back and draw in a breath through the nose.

161 THAI-STICK (1)

This is the most commonly used of the two variants listed.

162 THAI-STICK (2)

This sign, meaning TIE (neck), has the extended meaning of THAI-STICK for some younger Northern Californian signers.

FINGERSPELLED VOCABULARY

The following vocabulary was all fingerspelled by the Deaf consultants involved with the research for this book. Other signers may have signs for these. Letters to be fingerspelled are underlined individually.

F-163 A̲L̲C̲O̲H̲O̲L̲I̲C̲S̲ A̲N̲O̲N̲Y̲M̲O̲U̲S̲, A̲A̲

F-164 B̲A̲R̲ (2)

F-165 BLACK B̲E̲A̲U̲T̲I̲E̲S̲
Black is signed and Beauties is fingerspelled.

F-166 BLACK O̲U̲T̲ (4)
Black is signed and Out is fingerspelled. This is a direct translation from English and is probably used by Deaf people who are more English oriented.

F-167 B̲O̲G̲A̲R̲T̲
This term is used more by signers in the East.

F-168 CRANK
This term is used mostly in the West.

F-169 LSD, ACID

F-170 MDA

F-171 MDM

F-172 MESCALINE, MESC, PEYOTE

F-173 METHADONE

F-174 MORPHINE

F-175 OPIUM

F-176 SEEDS

F-177 7-UP

F-178 STASH

F-179 THC

F-180 VALIUM
Instead of fingerspelling, some signers in the East use a "V" handshape to make a sign, shaking it in a small side to side manner.

BIBLIOGRAPHY

Battison, R. 1978. *Lexical Borrowing in American Sign Language,* Silver Spring, Md.: Linstok Press.

De Santis, S. 1977. Elbow to Hand Shift in French and American Sign Languages. A paper presented at the NWAVE Conference, Georgetown University, October, 1977.

Klima, E. and U. Bellugi. 1979. *The Signs of Language,* Cambridge, Mass.: Harvard University Press.

Supalla, T. and E. Newport. 1978. How Many Seats in a Chair? The Derivation of Nouns and Verbs in American Sign Language, in P. Siple, ed., *Understanding Language Through Sign Language Research,* New York: Academic Press, 91-132.

Wilbur, R. 1979. *American Sign Language and Sign Systems,* Baltimore: University Park Press.

Woodward, J. 1973. Some Observations on Sociolinguistic Variation and American Sign Language, *Kansas Journal of Sociology* 9:2, 191–200.

Woodward, J. 1975. Variation in American Sign Language Syntax: Agent-Beneficiary Directionality, in R. Fasold and R. Shuy, eds., *Analyzing Variation in Language,* Washington, D.C.: Georgetown University Press, 303–311.

Woodward, J. 1976. Black Southern Signing, *Language in Society* 5, 211–218.

Woodward, J. 1979. *Signs of Sexual Behavior,* Silver Spring, Md.: TJ Publishers.

Woodward, J. and S. De Santis. 1977a. Negative Incorporation in French and American Sign Languages, *Language in Society* 6, 379–388.

Woodward, J. and S. De Santis. 1977b. Two to One it Happens: Dynamic Phonology in Two Sign Languages, *Sign Language Studies* 17, 329–346.

Woodward, J. and C. Erting. 1975. Synchronic Variation and Historical Change in American Sign Language, *Language Sciences* 37, 9–12.

Woodward, J., C. Erting, and S. Oliver. 1976. Facing and Hand(l)ing Variation in American Sign Language Phonology, *Sign Language Studies* 10, 43–51.

SIGN INDEX

The number given with each sign listing is the sign number, not the page number. When the letter "F" appears before this sign number, it means that it is listed under the heading FINGERSPELLED VOCABULARY located on pages 72 and 73. The words "(note only)" appear after index listings for which there is no illustration, but for which there is a descriptive reference in the "sign note".

A

AA	F-163
ACID	F-169
ADDICT (note only)	137
ADDICTED	56
ADM (note only)	127
ALCOHOL	31
ALCOHOLIC	1
ALCOHOLICS ANONYMOUS	F-163
AMPHETAMINES	48
ANGEL-DUST (1)	126
ANGEL-DUST (2)	127
APPREHEND (1)	128
APPREHEND (2)	129
APPREHEND(-GROUP)	130
ARREST (1)	128
ARREST (2)	129
ARREST(-GROUP)	130

B

BAD TRIP (note only)	81
BAR (1)	2
BAR (2)	F-164
BECOME-HEAVILY-INVOLVED-IN	57
BEER (1)	3
BEER (2)	4
BEER-CAN	5
BENNIES	48
BLACK-BEAUTIES	F-165
BLACK-OUT (1)	58
BLACK-OUT (2)	59
BLACK-OUT (3)	60
BLACK-OUT (4)	F-166
BLOODSHOT-EYES (1)	61
BLOODSHOT-EYES (2)	62
BOGART	F-167
BOMBED (1)	14
BOMBED (2)	15
BOMBED (3)	16
BONG	131
BOTTLE	6
BUST (1)	128
BUST (2)	129
BUST(-GROUP)	130
BUSTED (1)	128
BUSTED (2)	129
BUSTED (-GROUP)	130

C

CAFFEINE	33
CHAIN-SMOKE (1)	115
CHAIN-SMOKE (2)	116
CHAMPAGNE	7
CHEWING-TOBACCO (note only)	125
CHUG	10
CIGAR (1)	117
CIGAR (2)	118
CIGAR (3)	119
CIGARETTE (1)	120
CIGARETTE (2)	121
CLEAN-GRASS	86
COCA-COLA	34
COCAINE	132

COCKTAIL 8
COCKTAIL-PARTY 9
COFFEE 35
COKE (COCA-COLA) 34
COKE (COCAINE) 132
COKE-SPOON 158
COLUMBIAN 85
COLUMBIAN GOLD 85
COOK-HEROIN 133
COUGH (1) 63
COUGH (2) 64
CRANK F-168
CRYSTAL (1) 126
CRYSTAL (2) 127
CUT(-DRUGS-WITH-OTHER-SUBSTANCE) 134
CUT-HASH 135

D

DEAL(-IN-DRUGS) 136
DEALER (note only) 136
DEPRESSANT 38
DIET-PILLS 39
DIZZY (note only) 29
DO-YOU-WANT-TO-SMOKE-GRASS 87
DOPE (1) 95
DOPE (2) 96
DOPE (3) 97
DOWN-A-BOTTLE 10
DOWNERS 40
DRAFT-BEER 11
DRINK-A-SHOT 12
DRINK-LIQUOR 13
DRUG-DEPENDENCE (1) 65
DRUG-DEPENDENCE (2) 66
DRUG-HABIT 67
DRUGS 137
DRUNK (1) 14
DRUNK (2) 15
DRUNK (3) 16
DRUNK (noun) 17
DRUNKARD 17
DT's (note only) 70

E

F

FAINT (1) 58
FAINT (2) 59
FAINT (3) 60
FINISH-OFF-A-BOTTLE 18
FINISH-OFF-A-GLASS 18
FLASHBACK (1) 68
FLASHBACK (2) (note only) 70
FREAK-OUT 69

G

GLUE-SNIFFING 155
GRASS (1) 95
GRASS (2) 96
GRASS (3) 97

H

HALLUCINATE 70
HALLUCINOGENIC-DRUG 41
HANGOVER (note only) 13
HASH-OIL (1) 138
HASH-OIL (2) 139
HEAD-SHOP (note only) 147
HEAVY-GRASS-SMOKER (1) 100
HEAVY-GRASS-SMOKER (2) 101
HEAVY-SMOKER (1) 115
HEAVY-SMOKER (2) 116
HEROIN (1) 137
HEROIN (2) (note only) 153
HEROIN (3) (note only) 154
HIGH-FROM-DRUGS (1) 71
HIGH-FROM-DRUGS (2) 72
HIGH-FROM-DRUGS (3) 73
HIT 111
HOOKA 140
HOOKED-ON 56

HORSE (1)	137	MARIJUANA-PIPE	
HORSE (2) (note only)	153	(note only)	112
HORSE (3) (note only)	154	MDA	F-170
HYPODERMIC NEEDLE (1)		MDM	F-171
(note only)	153	MEDICINE	42
HYPODERMIC NEEDLE (2)		MESCAL	F-172
(note only)	154	MESCALINE	F-172
		METHADONE	F-173
		MIX-DRINKS	20
I		MIXED-DRINK	8
ILLICIT(-DRUG)-DEALINGS	141	MORPHINE	F-174
INCENSE	142	MUNCHIES	75
INSERT(-A-DRUG)-ANALLY	143		
		N	
J		NARC	145
JOINT (1)	88	NARCOTICS	137
JOINT (2)	89	NARCOTICS-OFFICER	145
JUNKIE (note only)	137		
		O	
K		O.D.	76
KILO	90	ON-THE-WAGON	21
		OPIUM	F-175
		OUNCE	146
L		OVERDOSE	76
LID (1)	91		
LID (2)	92	**P**	
LID-SIZE (PARTIAL)	94	PARAPHERNALIA	147
LID-SIZE (WHOLE)	93	PASS-JOINT-AROUND	99
LIQUEUR	19	PASS-OUT	22
LIQUOR	31	PCP (1)	126
LIQUOR-STORE (note only)	13	PCP (2)	127
LOADED	74	PEPSI	36
LSD	F-169	PEYOTE	F-172
LUSH	17	PILLS (1) (note only)	50
		PILLS (2) (note only)	51
		PILLS (3)	42
M		PLASTERED (1)	14
MAINLINE	144	PLASTERED (2)	15
MARIJUANA (1)	95	PLASTERED (3)	16
MARIJUANA (2)	96	POPPER	148
MARIJUANA (3)	97	POT (1)	95
MARIJUANA (4)	98	POT (2)	96

POT (3)	97	SMASHED (3)	16
POT-HEAD (1)	100	SMOKE-CIGARETTE	122
POT-HEAD (2)	101	SMOKE-GRASS	111
POT-PARTY	102	SMOKE-MARIJUANA-PIPE	112
PRESCRIPTION-DRUG	43	SMOKE-TOBACCO-PIPE (1)	123
PUSH(-DRUGS)	136	SMOKE-TOBACCO-PIPE (2)	124
PUSHER (note only)	136	SNIFF-GLUE	155
		SNORT	156

Q

		SNORT-A-LINE	157
QUAALUDES (1)	44	SNORT-FROM-SPOON	158
QUAALUDES (2)	45	SNORT-WITH-STRAW (1)	159
		SNORT-WITH-STRAW (2)	160
		SNORTING-SPOON	158

R

		SOBER	26
		SOCIAL-DRINKER	27
RAID	149	SPACED-OUT (1)	78
REDS	46	SPACED-OUT (2)	79
ROACH (1)	103	SPEED	48
ROACH (2)	104	STASH	F-178
ROACH-CLIP (1)	105	STIMULANT	49
ROACH-CLIP (2)	106	STIMULATE	49
ROACH-CLIP (3)	107	STONED (1)	113
ROACH-CLIP (4)	108	STONED (2)	114
ROLL-A-JOINT	109	STRAIGHT	80
ROLLING-PAPER	110		

T

S

		THC	F-179
SCALE (LARGE)	150	TAKE-PILL (1)	50
SCALE (SMALL)	151	TAKE-PILL (2)	51
SCOTCH	23	TEA	37
SCREWDRIVER	24	TEETOTALER	28
SEEDS	F-176	THAI-STICK (1)	161
SEVEN-AND-SEVEN	25	THAI-STICK (2)	162
SEVEN-UP	F-177	THROW-UP	83
SHOOT-UP (1)	152	TIPSY	29
SHOOT-UP (2)	153	TOBACCO	125
SHOOT-UP (3)	154	TOBACCO-PIPE (1)	
SICK-FROM-OVERDOSE	77	(note only)	123
SLEEPING-PILLS	47	TOBACCO-PIPE (2)	
SMACK (1)	137	(note only)	124
SMACK (2) (note only)	153	TOKE	111
SMACK (3) (note only)	154	TRANQUILIZERS	52
SMASHED (1)	14	TRIP (1)	81
SMASHED (2)	15	TRIP (2)	82

U

UPPERS   53

V

VALIUM   F-180
VODKA   30
VOMIT   83

W

WACK (1)   126

WACK (2)   127
WATER-PIPE   140
WEED (1)   95
WEED (2)   96
WEED (3)   97
WHISKEY   31
WHITES (1)   54
WHITES (2)   55
WINE   32
WINO   17
WITHDRAWAL-SYMPTOMS 84

X, Y, Z

PERSONAL NOTES

We encourage you to use this space for recording of signs and/or variations preferred by your local Deaf community.

82